ICEBERGS IN PARADISE

SAYAN BASAK

Woven Words Publishers OPC Pvt. Ltd.

Registered Office:

Vill: Raipur, P.O: Raipur Paschimbar,

Dist: Purba Midnapore, Pin: 721401,

West Bengal, India.

www.wovenwordspublishers.in

Email: editor@wovenwordspublishers.in

First published by Woven Words Publishers OPC Pvt. Ltd., 2017

Copyright© Sayan Basak, 2017

POETRY

IMPRINT: WOVEN WORDS FIRE

ISBN 13: 978-93-86897-11-4

ISBN 10: 9386897113

Price: ₹150/$8

This book is a work of fiction. All names, characters, places, addresses and incidents are fictitious and product of the author's imagination. Any resemblance with any events, locales, persons-living or dead, is purely coincidental.

The author asserts the moral right to be identified as the author of this work.

All rights reserved. This book is sold to the condition that it shall not, by way of trade or otherwise, be lent, resold, hired out, or otherwise circulated without the publisher's prior consent in any form of binding or cover other than that in which it is published and without a similar condition, including this condition, being imposed on the subsequent purchaser.

Printed and bound in India

Between your fear and my love ...

Seek for me
inside the fading fabric
of fallen fairies,
in stilly woven whispers
of murmuring morning mist,
as metaphors of a 'Madeleine moment'
susurrate opalescent drops
of a weeping winter,
among your humming heartbeats...

Weep for me
in nascent night-falls,
in ever dreamt galactic black holes,
while liquid pearls of silver silence
drip on your fossilized fibres...
and my alabaster absence
echoes across a *dim deja vu...*

Bleed for me
In redolent rhymes
of hitching heartbeats,
when limping oaths breed
crimson blood-beads
above the brunette breath
of vacillating vehemence,
and love drifts in translucent trance...
until your starving sighs' squandered chance
dissolves into
my star-dusty death

Witnessing

Rustling firs whispers
the moment's fragrant message,
as skies' deep blue patches
look down on me across
formless windows of
pine-needle foliage,
and a hell-bent tiny ant
climbs among the blonde hairs
of my lower arm.

Lukewarm breeze touches my skin;
a faraway cuckoo's song
break the dense, humming silence,
Descending onto the cool ground,
between the recumbent shapes of
yours and mine,
a rusty fur jumps from
branch to branch,
tasselled ears hark
our equable breathing,
a tossed cone falls on
your bare, outstretched leg,
while squirrels' pearl eyes
shine on us, and
tickling my elbow's bend...
the ant legs arrive to my upper arm.
Strayed sunbeams explode
behind my closed eyelids,
and a growing soft shadow
covers my face,
your body's warmth

engulfs my senses,
Only a fieldfare sings
Above the vibrating
touch of your nearing lips,
and the small, black ant
falls off from my uplifted, hugging arm.

Secrets

My secrets ache inside my bones
I despise them but they're mine to own
No one knows my shameful sins
It's just not safe to let them in

Only a sacred few know the truth
But soon they'll know because there's proof
It's written in black all across my face
My secrets are the kind you can never erase

My shame is like poison –
seeping through my pores,
The irrevocable fact that I'm a filthy ****
People will judge without knowing the facts
They will whisper and

point the odds are all stacked.
A black cloud will forever follow me around
The disgust will overwhelm me
until I drown
How am I supposed to go on
with this cancer?
Please let me know 'cause
I don't know the answer.

And I miss you ...written in red

Liquid moonbeams dream
silvery quietude over the
depths of our indigo lake,
while falling instants fade in
time's alabaster maze,
like soft, opalescent ghosts
get lost in whispering haze,
and love's artistically curved,
throbbing shades, engulf our shapes ...

I weave my sighs' crystal lace
between the dimples of your auburn face,
Drawing starry smiles
around your maroon eyes,
lifted up by your kiss
Into the diamond spheres
of our seraphic breath...

And,
the scintillate scent of velvet skies
fills up our lungs from far...
afar...
And we merge
Slowly... within a shooting star.

Like classically composed scherzo of sun rays...

Remember...
summertime crickets
dreamt their silver pizzicato,
the lake shore's nocturnal adagio
merged with our ruby kiss,
as we smiled, engulfed by
the background music of
diamond moon rays,
you whispered ...
we can't part, but the
bargain takes place
storms in between'

And the crescendo of your
Masculine symphony
turned into harmony
Within the newly found
cadence of
my silently rippling feminity.

Now,
lightning's explode
upon a basso timpani,
the rampaging lake's dissonances
rage this way
over the un-tuned horizon,
while our rain drenched sheet-music
drowns in clouded cacophony,
And your torn, silvery strings
vibrate in dissonant dolour,

I say ...
hold on,
I won't let go of your hand,
my inseparable part'
And, we await the
classically composed
scherzo of sun rays,
you and I,
hidden within the notes
of our Amaranthine love.

A late-night origami ...

Look sweetie,
as my nimble fingers
are folding an
own-hand-made origami,
your playful imagery is
hidden between the
plies of placation;
your hoarse voice
crayons the pattern,
while my every motion
nears to the artistic outcome,
my pink paper turns into
more and more sensitive
during the work of art,
and the folded masterpiece
appears after the last ply...

Your face adorns my joy,
as the artwork
breeds its well-deserved prize ...

Close your eyes, sweetie,
you'll catch a flashing glimpse of the inspired creating,
while you are sleeping.

As you grew up within me...and we fade into the starry skies

Diamond dew drops
shattered in our love's liquid fire,
bare sighs bloom this way
beneath quivering sun rays,
while bitter pearls
rolled freely from your
childhood's pristine ocean,
to meet me ...

Our morning
became to noon,
as the leaden mask melted
from your seraphic cheeks,
drip by drip,
And, your inner
little boy
dissolved into my
nourishing motherhood ~

Flaming rubies adorned our afternoon,
And we sucked bleeding drops
Of honey lust auburn moans
echoed between your Amaranthine lips,
I bit your kiss
in our fireworks' exploding bliss,
And collapsed with
goose bumps along
my nakedly curved
marble spine ...

Torn pieces of time
grew dim within my eyes,
while we hid ourselves inside
love's throbbing chambers, silently ...
And your inner teenager
merged into my fertile feminity.

Gold evening glinted
Above the shores of your
nearly lost limpidity,
we walked barefoot,
with softly scattered
silky steps, among
the shards of your
nacreous inner truth ...
I shot the silver bullets
of my crystal words into the
undersea monster of your
blood-sucking lies,
then we stared ...
in *deep* silence ...
as nascent moonbeams
whispered silvery sobriety
above our new-born verity.

Velvet night unfolds
Beyond the threshold,
perfume of freedom
permeates our
resurrected truth,
my exhaled breath
fills up your pulsating lungs,

And your heartbeat
throbs inside my veins,
as we stand ...this way ...
surrounded by opalescent silence,
entwined in crimson palpitation ...
the only path leads upward,
it's time for us to start ...

I hide my sighs
into your embracing arms,
and we fade into the
starry skies.

Bridging the Gap

The room crowded
all doing their thing
parading impressive
to the other

Too close
and you are drinking
the next reveller's
beverage

Too distant
and no possibility
for contact, connection
and a changed life

Music blasting
rhythm changing
from pop to jazz
to rock

Ambience morphing
with each tune
ebb and flow
like a tidal wave
changing course
with the position
of moon

Bodies swaying
drinks flowing
uninhibited

with one spitting growl
losing it
by the third vodka

Others drowning toxic
in the inebriation
of their desires
closing the gap
between objects of interest
leaving little comfort zone
for the possibility
of saying NO

A fine line
between welcome mat,
healthy space
and shades of grey
in between

Anguish

The darkness seeps in through the cracks
the cracks are caused by all my pain
disdain is running through my veins
years of fear and dried up tears
I dread the things I haven't seen
I long for who I could have been
dismayed, betrayed, and full of shame
I try to change but stay the same
I play with words I've felt and heard
and contemplate things most absurd
behind my eyes inside my mind
pain and darkness you will find.

Dystopian Winds

Battle, Friction, Transition, all commence.
the wind interrogates -
Bullying its way into
the folds of her coat, and
Channelling its unwelcome fingers
through her hair.
The Free Lady walks on.
Frayed puppet strings, flung and torn
Whistle past her ear -
A synthetic song: made at a time
not long ago,
But similarly, an age away,
Is extracted from ears, replaced by the sound
of whirring klaxons from loudspeakers.
The lies sung before are drowned
in the sea of darkness
where the albatross flies in red.
The Free Lady does not halt.

In a bitten tree,
The sinews of a community
Rip, tear, and shred them on the jagged bark:
A knife-edge over which
The airs of Liberty are placed –
The Free Lady does not see, hear.

Dark clouds roll to meet her.
She is naked in defence -
The storms flow outside the teacups,
Twisting in wicked time
With the blaring of the future song -

"A warning!" - too late!
The free lady is cut.

Her free blood spilt,
The cold concrete shows no mercy
on her body.
An ugly stain is purged with
The same Mechanical Efficiency
That tightened its grip as we spoke.

The Fairy Gathering

In the shadows of the dark forest
In the afternoon waning light
The faeries are a gathering
To celebrate the night

In the wind I can hear them singing
Like the tinkling of bells
As clear as silver raindrops
Gently falling on the dells

I long to see them dancing
Underneath the silver moon
So, I sit among the shadows
And I offer them a tune

I heard them whisper in the trees
Laughter echoes in the glen
But they melt away like stardust
Far beyond all mortal ken

Lovelies in Pink

Oh! I can write,
and ode to the beauty you adorn in this shade.
Pen down lines to breathe a hymn to your luxurious grace.
But devoting words
sans voices to fall short of
Such wondrous gaze,
Is not my wish…
But habits make haste.

You are lovely in pink
is all I want you to know.
And, as silence to secrecy it suits you so That in every
moment of you, my heart elates,
Burning joyous with such fervour!
I am not alone to adore you,
yet don't count among the numerous confessions,

But if letters could speak and stand witness
Of how often they'd bled for your sake, Perhaps then...But
this is not their transgression.

Of subtle delights are your crimson lips Crashing hearts
with their fickle moods,
In adoration of pink, chaos ensues stirring little hidden
Armageddon.
And to smile at me, like you know
What goes on in my head.
Hearing what I mean but failed to say,
The words I mince and those I refrain,
Like you've known it all; have heard it all,
Until it passes on to the next of us.
Such salvation I regret.

That stark brilliance of raven hair,
Descend like bows of sable Linn Plummeting in depths of my lyrical affair
to merge with the secrets of your frame,
In crust of lustrous satin pink.
And my eyes, flustered and little out of breath,
Fixed between decency and allure, they Explore audacious curves to limn in praise And, hastily memorise but lose their way, And, fall short of things to say.

But it's the nature of your embodiment,
in this lighter hue of red; unfettered, unforgiving, unconquered, ever enticing,
Is a treacherous quest of what you are.

And finally, The careless joy in your rest,
That carries you to your faraway prince.
For his hidden lowe, you leave us be,
But asleep, would you ever see
How I steal a little of his pleasure,
To write in my poetic sins.

But you do look lovely in this shade,
And paper words will keep it safe.

The Contest

There is a battle I'll reveal
between two sides that want the same
happiness sought to fulfil
the breadth of life in expanse

There's a brawl between soldiers
one below and one above
contending for the common ground
exacting ruin with each stroke

Weaponized by good intent
the conflict wracks internal space
disrupting breath that I desire
choosing paths beyond the now

Each engaged in my employ
taking turns to steer the course
if only they would pull as one
provoking calm instead of strife

Drawing blood with each stroke
first the reason, then ardour
I'll never know which is best
a thousand scratches on my soul

The same master requests both
to make peace instead of war
pull together against a world
that cares little for this contest

Between the head and the heart
there's a battle every day
happiness should be the goal
if the contest was not a duel.

A Decision of Nothing

Witching hour approaches
the deliberation of today
becoming deadline of tomorrow
still with no insight
about which way to lean

The pot stirs
in the maelstrom
of uncertainty
so much riding
on so little

Every angle explored
crevice uncovered
rock turned over
in the hope of seeing
with clarity
that which is opaque

Finally, a decision is reached
agony over
guts spent
let's make it work

With time unfolding
we gaze at others
in similar quandary
who made the other choice
and they turned out ok too

Angst arises
pondering how much of life
spent deliberating

over the meaningless
for fear

Turning down the wrong alley
which emerges
as just another road
leading to the same place

Lost in A-minor dreams

Silent solitude of A-minor dreams,
like breathing loneliness in exhausted   phantasies' softly
woven death, now gleams in my iridescent iris, limpid

Chords of sonic constellations behind
the aesthetically chiselled ribs of
an alive musical instrument, blind
fibres of seer cells, sinking in mauve

Meditation, while intertwined sounds weep
liquid silence beneath my eyelashes,
drip by drip in time's heartbeats, still and
deep,
like kisses, merged in our missed embraces.

In echoing visions of your presence
I'm lost... without you... there's no existence.

Describing joy

Joy fell on an autumn kiss.
Bare feet dance in windswept fields
Where daisies fade, their seed drops,
Frolic with light breezes,
land in new places,
Take root, wait to germinate,
kissing the ground.

Joy fell on an autumn kiss.
Bare feet wander rows of
Corn, squash, and pumpkin.
Hands aid in harvest,
Baking, meal preparation,
Holding hands for grace.

Joy fell on an autumn kiss.
Bare feet splash cold water of lake
Birds call from tall pines letting me know
We have disturbed their peace.
Autumn leaves wave summer goodbye,
Floating on crisper winds.

Funeral of the day

Patterns of the wind,
shifting in the pale floor;
the soft, careless hands of twilight's colour
caressing the sands,
gracefully crafting hills and dells;
while the blue tongue of the sea
surges forward.

Lady Moon
awaits the death of Sun;
Her feathery feet
treading on the cool sands-
her snow-white raiment,
rippling with moonlight-pearls,
glowing with faerie light.

The night's black ink
caught in the prism of her eyes,
set in the shadows of her milky brow
between her elegant locks;
the dark coals
flickering across the blue heavens,
her dusky realm tonight;

Nature's palette-
smeared with swirling spectrums,
the dispersing crimson hues, the blood
of the tangerine Sun,
sinking slowly
into hissing waters.

The bleeding waves
slapping across the face of their slayer,

wombing across its fires.
Smoke rises from the red sea,
as water battles with flame.
The fleeting light is sucked
from every bloom,
and flickering candle,
and sealed in the chest of sea.

The funeral of the day
marches down the sea
to honeycombs in deeps;
and into Nature's arms, the Sun
returns once more to sleep.

Her Letters

Her yellow dandelion letters
of an intimate friendship,
began over coffee cups
with smiley faces on them.

Her amaranth pink letters
so full of charm with a touch of lace,
makes me blush without her
ever knowing that she did.

Her red garnet letters
commitment rang the bells of truth,
embedded with consequences
they fiddle throughout my mind
realizing what devotion meant;

Her green sage letters
immersed in jealousy,
inked in contentment
growing soiled seed
of a murky conscience .

Her black sable letters
gazing back at me
addressing me in impact font
waiting for me to sign…
Her letters

Stampede of Emotions

Stampede of emotions
knocked at my front door,
I let them in

A furious sea gushed
toppling history
escape breaths failed

Gathering gales just to blow
not limited to puffy cloud-like poofs

Quaking monumental exhales
tsunami sized sails
bellowed uncontrolled

Anchored swells
grounded deep within
roared

Tumbling alive the master of illusions
unbolted growls pounced free
Abandoning walls of clarity
chimes snapped double-time

No warning, no ceiling,
unstoppable
unlike me

How do you grab the tail
of a tornado and not let go?

Pacing couldn't resolve
this sudden surge to rise 'n fall
unveiling this wayward ghost

Fragmented disbelief lay
scattered underfoot
remnants disarrayed
white to ashen soot

Lines drenched, purred
too blurred to piece back together

Words seared in licks
scarred by insignificance.

Then the door blew closed

a single knob twist
unsalvageable debris
felled ringing

The stranger was me

The Curl of your Arms

Are peace-making,
when the burden is glorious
and the carnage, stilled

Yarrow blossoms,
where air loses light,
and mountain gloam
expose a sweetening rim

As worlds take,
give and disappear,
our bedded bones seed into morning,
silent as nocturnal rivers

There, you are as yet
an unidentified landscape of promise,
tucking beauty into horizon's age-hung face;

Charcoal sketches,
brightening in a curl of arms

The Moment in Time

To become separate from time
and in its enwrapping,
as Reality always,
now

It is a moment, in time
waiting for mind engaged with what is eternal
from the internal possibly infinite

Sight of what is of this worlds' ephemeral
and that, image of only
of what has been and will always be,
difference between life and Life

The moment
that is crossroad ahead in a life's living
choice of path possible,
man of time, man of eternity and so
decision of what's important of life
and priority

The Untold Valentine

Her eyes sparkled heart shaped lips so red, Hair silky blond corn silk down her back they said.
Body to die for voice of velvet cream,
She was poison to the soul every mans dream.

At the motel just at the edge of town,
she hung about a street lamp.
Beams of moon glow filtered through her hair,
yet from her fingertips blood dripped yet no one was aware
.

As the street lamp flickered her form faded in and out,
like an old movie worn and the voice crackled instead of a shout.
Those nearby saw not the evil there within reach,
that is until the strike of midnight another morsel she would feed.

Beckoning the strangers to bid them a good time,
Hips ever so shapely like a valentine.
Her eyes would beckon them drawing them near,
as she ran her fingers through their hair and whisper do not fear .

As she drug them out of the street lamp where darkness fell,
eyes wide open no longer a beauty they saw pure hell.
Mouth on mouth they couldn't scream as she fed,
exhuming their soul as their eyes wept.

Body losing form arms and legs limp without life,
eyes bulging from their sockets in fright.
Evil comes in many forms beauty is number one,

so beware of the shapely valentines they may be a loaded gun.

The Visitor

Broken nibs,
Stolen pencils,
Sneaking chocolates,
Screams for ice creams,
These were all-
The troubles she knew.
Until that day,
When he came.
Her dad's dear friend,
He did things new.
It was unlike,
The warmth she knew.
She cried for reasons,

None understood.
Had those fevers,
No drugs cured.
Mighty night mares,
Hugs couldn't help.
'Ghost, he must be!',
She told herself.
All she knew was,
She should hide…
Every time,
A visitor came…

Valentine's Library

Imagine if I was given one moment,
just a single slice of my past.
I could hold it close forever,
and that moment would always last.
I'd put the moment in a safe,
within my hearts abode.
I could open it when I wanted,
and only I would know the code.

I could choose a time of laughing,
a time of happiness and fun.
I could choose a time that tried me,
through everything I've done.

I sat and thought about what moment,
would always make me smile.
One that would always push me,
to walk that extra mile.

If I'm feeling sad and low,
if I'm struggling with what to do.
I can go and open my little safe,
and watch my moment through.

There are moments I can think of,
that would lift my spirits every time.
The moments when you picked me up,
when the road was hard to climb.

For me to only pick one moment,
to cherish, save and keep,
Is proving really difficult,
as I've gathered up a heap!

I've dug deep inside my heart,
found the safe and looked inside,
there was room for lots of moments,
in fact hundreds if I tried.

I'm building my own little library,
embedded in my heart,
for all the moments spent with you,
before you had to part.

I can open it up whenever I like,
pick a moment and watch it through,
My little library acts as a promise,
I'll never ever forget you

As We Once Were

You lay with the window open wide,
the curtains licking the air.
Two bodies merged as one,
entwined in limbs, sweat and wind,
bedraggled breaths roll from your throat.

I watch as you press your pink fleshy lips to his.
Your head dipping habitually to where his hand rests on your shoulder.

The smile spreads slowly across your face as he strokes your cheek with an outstretched forefinger.

You take it in your mouth, as though it were a stick of rock.

Sweet as honey,
as sweet as the grin that emblazons your face.

A lone strand of hair sticks to your glistening forehead.
He moves it with a stroke of his hand, as though this small act of love were nothing to him.
Your eyes widen as you press your body against his,
biting your lower lip, as if this ecstasy were about to make you burst.

He looks away, the wind blowing through his hair; Mr Cool.
You grab his crotch
craving his attention.
It is yours now.
Oh, lucky you.

Enjoy it while you can my love.
For neither of you will see tomorrow.
You will both become dust, trapped in the wind,
blowing through an open window into a room of treachery.

Call Me When You're Sober

Fall leaves sweep by
Caught in the cool gusts of wind
Dancing coyly around an old pair of denim jeans
Walking briskly towards the graveyard
A cigarette tossed upon the ground
Huddle around the warmth
of the last dying embers
Laughing at the irony
in holding hands, shivering
Neck is sore, from lack of weight on shoulders
A 5 o'clock shadow covering
where the traces of a smile still linger
Pleading forward tongue

Grasping Mexico at the hems of her dress
Pleading for the irony to return
Swept back the phoenix
in bright orange hair
with pale limbs, unrestrained
Unrestricted, swim across campus
in thrift store vintage attire
Incite doctrine with the sound of sneakers
upon the pavement.

Just Before Autumn

After the fog lifted, sunlight dappled through an ancient curtain,
a slow revelation, yet only silence remained.
I found repose by the north side of the house
where only moss felt safe enough to grow; deep, lush, damp,
a thickened brush of emerald heavy near four symmetrical cherry trees,
long before Pablo found me (or I found him),
I knew the taste and texture of melancholy,
the feeling of an ocean surging inside the caverns of my heart.
On the south side, two imposing pear trees stood;
hornets would gather there, greedily gathering fallen fruit's waste,
waiting to insert their barbed stingers into the tender foot of a child

who would not weep, who would only mourn
their sudden, terrible demise.

Midnight Undressed

Only trust mother
as she passes in a grain of sand
and fleck of moonlight spilling through our fingertips
into a thousand blessings of warmth amid winter's wanton
viscosity

She is made of butterflies, and dragons,
angel wings
slowly vanishing into her own recipe
of corrosive, sweetened evil
Beckoning
the spider's incantation to spill from between my lips
twist and contort the steel and silk
strings for dark marionettes
to manipulate you
Into the perfect girl
slip headfirst into death
just like a favourite dress

Know, the game we play in life is lost
and the consequence is a thick, black liquid substance
crude oil
filling your lungs, your eyes, ears and mouth
until the truth becomes a foul taste
and condolences hollow, handed freely to the masses in
place their daily bread
they've been filled to the brim
with impotent gestures encased in pretty pockets of air

The stomach always turning cogs of reason
into something anything
To flee the night's raging tempest

pounding and grinding skulls into the concrete shrieking,
screaming, and battering against some flimsy hope
scantily clad and emaciated, labelled 'faith'

'There is nothing here for you.
no one for you.
you are all alone.'
To be murdered softly, slowly
by the inches

Our tormentor
indifferent to age's brutal cruelty
un-noticing of the victim's corpse rotting
its way back home
into the earth

We are orphaned and offered up
into the night in sacrifice to
a vacancy large enough for one hundred million man-made-gods
to live comfortably and somewhere still
out there
one wanders keeping our secrets safe
from us

We are unclaimed
wasted
what little worth we may have unravelling
before our very eyes
like cheap fabric
in the mirrors of the mind

A wisp of black smoke
acrid and already
beginning to evaporate

A fate shared by all known things
amid these gargantuan halls
of universal secrecy
with frowns locked and written in the stars
we are blinded by the fire and ruined by the storm
before we touch our hearts desire
and etch it into form

Yet still we cling to these forbidden sheets
of darkness
under the birth right of this
lonely star
wrapped around our throat
tighter and tighter
panic reigns, is running wild

seeking annihilation of resolve
as anger, fear,
our questions, and confusions
rattle off into the heavens like falling rocks
over a cliff
only to return to us
not in the form of an echo,
but folded neatly
in an envelope
which reads:

'No such address.'

Innuendo

Inside the old place,
Shrieking could be heard,
the epic rumour had it
that she roamed the halls,

Stinky, smouldering smell,
was all that was left
of the lady of house,
they found charcoal

sitting beside the door,
and in the burnt embers,
he was at the local bar
when she was poisoned,

when he came home
he went straight to bed,
her skin, red like a bloom,
but drunk, he had an alibi,

a year later he was found
drunk with his skin bright red,
like a bad sunburn, alive,
later died in the hospital

Inhibited

remember how the delicate fabric traced the edges of my skin
how your fingers followed the steams as they stitches through the cotton layers
the way your eyes gleamed into mine
and my heart beat for the tender embrace that came with your kiss
your lips met mine with a rough touch
and my mind took an unsettling seat
my heart in the moment, my mind lost in your beating chest
the world took a seat as our bodies and minds collided into each other
and while everything else faded into the backdrop
our bodies settled onto your sheets

sitting alone in my bed, the fan blowing against my skin
I remember the rush of your breath on my cheek as we layed there entangled in each other
the body heat the only thing between us.

now between us lies everything that once held us together
a void has formed between our lips and her beauty between our minds

I still remember the inseparable bond that stitches us together like two pieces of cloth
now the stitches have loosened and the thread traces the ground as it falls from us

our sheets of fabric go their separate ways

you flow precariously through the breeze as your strings tie
you onto her
and I brush through the wind and into the river

Water-diamonds.

He feels at home behind the glass, in the glass as a
waterless ice cube,
feet swimming into soft mouths of pillows. A warm shape
of plastic
he palms as a pair of breasts, my breasts in this breezy room
an island he sits as I curl smooth on mine like a fancy
groove
of new pool, and we share the same fruits, last names, tall
kisses

Smoke hangs silently outside in abstract shapes as artists
draw from their lips
then they climb back up the steps, my heart naked on the
couch
like an open bag of chips they munch my pulse whole as
almonds,
soft crunches tucked deep behind their bellies

His fingers weave sweet Nicotine through my big brown
bouquet of hair
I loathe it but I love him and the scent that lulls my nose to
dreams

Our sleepless eyes starless and glowing like highlighter
juice,
carry feathers of conversations on cinnamon-winged
tongues
as I slide, a wet bird into the sheets of my quill and explode

Then he caresses my words from afar
with ears clearer than shallow water-diamonds

and we swim off,
a pair of knitted goldfish
in the silk of night.

Rapt

I discovered poetry
in the creases of your mouth,
every line a verse that tasted
of midnight's burning fire.

Laid out under paddling stars
as lips swept over mine,
I heard those silken stanzas
as lushly painted kisses.

And I danced as waltzing fingertips
serenaded lightly over skin,
my strands of hair snuggled gently
into the folding of your palm.
I listened to the thunder
as it roared its passion
in the pounding of my lungs,
spilling breaths across your cheekbones
under slowly lowering lids.

Every cursive letter that fell upon my edges
filled my eyes with wonder,
my mouth with hungered need
and I swallowed pastel murmurs
swept light from inside cheeks,
as tongues whispered poems
in the tingling touch of tips.

And all along the curve of hips
I felt the beauty of your love,
my bend of back replying

to the words inside your sighs.

And still I lay beside you
within the journals of my mind,
writing poetry in images
of days spent wrapped inside your art

Caffeinated inks

the ink that flows, ebbing and pulsating
ever so slightly, vacillating between words
forming and deforming figures of birds
coffee as it pours, out your head
another day
as it impales the thin curtain,
a few dust crystal go past
into the room without asking,
they explore the little untidy bed
crumpled with sheets, dappled with ink blots

its ink or coffee that runs
both in the room above the gritty street
and in the clotted beats, of heart beats
fading

mixing aromas of the two fluids,
memories float in sight
the steam runs on stream of
rising ideas as they're flung
in the harsh winter night

the hot fumes intertwine,
they express a love, I couldn't
through the ink…
and the inklings died stifled

vestiges of mists now float
on the shores of my coffee
far too cold to drink,
too bitter are the memories

Seeing Green

She felt tension in rambunctious blood,
leaking through tenuous veins,
as bitter bones revolted;
she experienced the horror from the previous night,
how he took off his belt and thundered,
slapping that menace across satin skin,
all because the gravy was lumpy.

She had endured this kind of assault before,
but she was no longer a sucker for unpredictable behaviour,
like the time at the gazebo,
where he shoved her in the lake, the water
soaking her silk gown, ruined
by the stale water from the mud and mulch,
not comprehending what she had done to deserve
such a heinous reaction from him.
Later he would justify his behaviour declaring
that he had insisted
she wear red instead of green
since most of the other ladies
would wear the same colour;
after all, she didn't want to show off
and stand out needlessly.

He had proposed just three weeks prior, his romanticism
displayed as he whisked her away in a helicopter
as it whirled though Blue Mountains,
and a thousand lakes.
She had agreed to take his hand that night,
but new information suggested
that he was one to be wary,

as she placed the ring
in its rightful case, grabbed her suitcase,
as she packed her clothes,
took some mementos, just for her,
left the keys on the bed,
without a note or letter,
and fled for freedom.
As the taxi drove her to the airport, she caught
the noon plane back to her family and friends
who would ensure this monster
would not terrorize her
one last time

Scattering ashes

the dark roses were carmine with blood
as they lay on the light grey ashes.
the snow-stained earth received them both
in the morning, silent but for the occasional cry
of the crematorium cat

the air was too cold for scent to penetrate,
and the occasional snowflake flurry
cast tiny fragments over
the red-gray resting place
Unsheltered from the sun, wind, rain and snow
the flowers and ashes lay exposed together
and only the name remains as a marker
dry as a desert you lie there,
cold as the snow capping a mountain peak,
and only the fragile beauty of dust
remains for a brief time
before the winds scatter it,
the rains wash it away,
the sun dries it out
and the eternal frost
Shrouds it

Full moon musings

Despite dark curtains tightly drawn
and accumulating layers of clouds,
the full moon does a good job of
keeping me awake.

I roll on my back to snuggle
into comfort, extend legs
and arms, sink my head
in between pillows.

Once again you visit
my restless contemplation
of maybes and
missed possibilities.

Eyes unable to close
on those unreachable landscapes
where you linger, beguiling smile
on your pensive face,
I listen to faint night noises,
trying to catch your step,
the turn of your key—
but you never come

The caged bird's song

The lark sets free when morning chimes
the cast of ribcage breaks,
in melodies of dawning rhymes
the tears of night she makes

In haste she flies seeking respite
with winds upon her breast,
beneath the blessed sun so bright
She bends the throttle west.

Through roaring clouds and thunderstorms
she braves for clearer skies,
a flutter fly seldom performs
to boost her drowning sighs,

from soaring heights she gazes down,
green meadows, blooms delight,
butterflies in honeyed brown
dance happily alright.

When eve becomes and day is done
she's miles and miles from home,
the burden of the setting sun
that sets the doldrums hum,

to barren ground she tumbles down
succumbed to one more night,
nowhere to go and broken down
she trudges back in plight,

the hollowness of metal ribs

that beckoned her along,
on lonely nights she softly croons
the caged bird's mourning song.

Pinkly swears

our breath smelled like gumballs
and we took turns counting
freckles on the other's nose
it was summer before second-grade, 2013
we were best friends forever, Rema and I
two peas in matching pigtails and polyester
Bonded by pinkly swears
we hung upside down from her maple tree
squished footprints in mud
along the edge of her front yard pond
laid in thick grass for hours
whispering how we wanted to
kiss Scottie Desun behind
the big playground sliding board
because he was the cutest boy in school
we answered all the important questions
seven-year-old girls have
with daisy petals and magic 8-balls
made wishes on shooting stars and
fallen lashes
and I used to wish most of all
that my eyes could be the same
shade of blue as hers
it was like god himself cut out tiny
circles of sky
we spent every weekend together
on bicycles and horseback
danced together, skipped arm-in-arm
chased butterflies through wildflowers
beside her pasture field
discovered the beauty in flight

and the significance of wings
she was absent from school when
her dad called my dad that Friday evening
me, busily packing my holly hobby
suitcase
some kind of flu, they thought and
we would surely play together the following
Saturday
she collapsed in the driveway, riding her bike
an aneurysm burst in her brain
she died in her mother's arms, in the rough
gravel, her blue eyes open, staring heavenward
she was seven
and we were best friends forever
when my youngest daughter was born, she had
those same eyes, carved from a summer sky
it was a hot July day that we brought her home
from the hospital, sat her car seat on the picnic table
as family gathered around to meet her and almost
immediately, the most beautiful brandies butterfly paused
on my shoulder, fluttering, as if to remind me of
the beauty found in blue and
the significance of wings

Thin Ice

This is about making excuses.
We made our way down to the frozen lake,
over the slick rock steps
to the slant of wood that connected the overhang to the dock.
We clung to its frozen wet rail,
which bit at our gloveless fingers,
yet supported us on the steep decline.
Swing dancing, and at
the haunted house.
I chased you on the playground,
and you listened to my fears.
and worried as our feet forgot us. If we slipped
we'd plummet into the water.
We leapt
You shared
my secret.
from the dock, onto the rocky shore, barricaded by the steep cliff,
littered with climbing vines and coke cans.
You can be so oblivious.
There, we collected rocks,
and experimented,
launching and flinging them over the ice.
You shifted.
Some hopped a few times, others exploded to dust and pebbles,
as others impaled themselves in the surface,
stuck sideways,
sticking in the water
and sticking out.

I guess you didn't know any better.
The big rocks sank right through the ice,
not a single icy crack left behind,
only rock-prints in their stead.
You grew up faster than I did,
and left me trailing in your dust. You
Water gurgled up through the holes and
the air bubbles beneath the ice
seemed to flee from me,
far from me,
and to an anti-you.
swam from hole to hole like stingrays,
fanning out their fins.
Perhaps I imagine, or overreact,
but you boarder the unrecognizable.
causing other holes to cough and spurt.
you used to be wonderfully naïve,
but no more
We went to the high dock, too.
You promised you wouldn't forget me.
I begged you to promise again, but
That was the hardest part.
One of us heaved a boulder to the upper deck and
hurled it from the edge.
I shifted too.
It left a magnificent imprint.
We laughed
It's difficult to readjust.
until we saw the fish,
stiff and white,
float up to the surface with the air bubbles.
We paused
This is about coping.

and laughed again,
only different this time.

Candle Wind

Warm wind trickling down my back,
tracing my spine,
rippling my shirt with colourful fingertips,
playfully brushing through my hair
candle wind
candlelight pulsing airily inside our in closed palms
clutching the hard wax
like holding tiny stars to brighten the fading daylight,
crisp smiles with peppermint teeth,
exploding our hands across the grass surface,
smelling the summertime candles

Clouds wrapping around the moon,
glowing around the soft white powder
collapsing in silence,
fireworks crack across the sky in calculated dances
we gaze in breathless huddles around the flickers of light

images of fireworks dancing across our mouths,
kissing in the smell of vanilla
cuddled under your coat,
sunlight dancing in pink colours across the sea,
salt covered trees bending towards the candle wind

Tonight, we flow in an unwritten rhythm,
candles lighting up our bad intentions,
teenagers floating high in the parks,
dancing underneath exploding moons and stars
kissing candles

I look at you behind the glass

I look at you behind the glass.
You are otherworldly, alien
in your stillness, but of course
you are human, thinned out man,

skin rippling inwardly like a gill,
malfunctioning gill, calling me
into your body. The pale pill
of your large organ flesh has made
you the odd colour of your own eyes,
which have been adjusted, which are absent,
so I'm missing the element of your reflection.
I want your eyes, the steel grey-blue,
your eyes that once became an obdurate bubble
as I looked into them like a telescope through
a round submarine whose mission was to find
something more than the matter of dry earth.

There, I saw water, the way its gradient
moved, translucent to an opaque dark, the way
strange fish lit up, the way that light
reminded us of home coming back, that heaven
we were always told to believe in; the portrait
of Jesus and his wingspan arms behind the same light,
light which has never seen the land, for it might
dissolve into the free-moving air or our hands.
Now your fish light, unexplainably exotic,
is diluted, nearly invisible, in the way of Jesus'
eyes, tightening my body like a muscle uncertain
of its function, clambering for motion,
and here I am, poking your glass box like a child at the zoo

watching the animals, but instead I'm watching you,
blue, beneath the barrier with no great escape.
Your sea, no sea at all. This place, no place

Lovers, Till the End

traveling down memory lane
we forgot our despises
as we enjoy the moment we mingle together on the train
a stroke of luck which has put our love of old
within the reach of one other yet again
now what should never have been
flourishes yet again
like a Georgia Peach in the swelter of summer
growing with every clicky click of the rail
then the conductor calls last stop
their eyes lost in wonderment
and they are now as they were then
Lovers, Till the End

Nature

The fading light of setting sun
Sinks slowly into purple seas
It's rays suffused between the shrouds
Of gold and bitter orange clouds,
The outlined silhouetted trees,
And Venus on the edge of night
Beguiling all with silver light.

The mountain peaks bedecked in snow,
Their fir trees droop with loaded bough,
The frozen brook all cloaked in mist
Awaits the springtime's gentle kiss.
A snow fox passes softly now.
Yet buried deep and slumbering,
The seeds and bulbs of nascent spring.

Beneath the rainforest canopy
Bejewelled with the fallen drops,
The orchids riot in their hues
Of yellow, orange, reds and blues,
The mating chorus never stops
A panoply in shades of green,
A thousand creatures heard, unseen.

As children we all understood
That nature should be held in awe,
We laid and stared at clouds and skies,
We celebrated butterflies
And so respected nature's law.
Why is it we cannot see how
The Earth needs us to do that now?

Alkonost

Tailed voices echo through the stubborn cove;
gently simmering repetitive chords that coat
the thick fog that lingers-- The sweet scented
breath runs its tongue against your heart;
and in you are reeled, at death shall you part.

The fine strands of thick feathers, glisten against
the water's skin, as fine golds lactate and shimmer
the heat that lies within. Come closer, catch a glimpse
that will so wickedly fade. Catch the Siren song as
it beckons amongst the splintered rocks, at commands
obeyed.

For once a man stole integrity, of a bird so wild and so free;
the feathered wings dismantled and grounded shall stay we-
for temptation is, beyond all accounts, the wicked face of
greed.
We take your breath from watered mouths,
and slip away
silently
beyond the sea

Sweet Wish

A small little girl,
all alone,
runs into a field searching for treasures untold.
With a subtle sway, her eyes widen,
as her gaze comes across a dandelion.

Slowly she walks towards it,
as if it was a dream.
She sits upon her knees,
staring at it revertly.
Carefully, she reaches towards it.

The smooth surface of the stem
convinced her she wasn't just imagining
the sacred relic before her eyes.
With a tender smile,
she let a gentle sigh.

With only a mother's kind of care,
from the ground, did she sweetly tear
the white and green genie
from it's
earth-bound snare.

She closed her eyes
and made her wish.
The feathery petals did she kiss
before she let out a gentle blow,
allowing the seeds to go free.

A warm, kind smile lit up her face

as she stood up with practiced grace.
Her quiet steps led her from this meadow
and to a small cottage
her entire countance mellow.

She sadly watched the people inside,
but to her surprise, they did not cry.
Laughter reigned as they all remembered the happy times together.
She grinned and turned,
her entire body faded away, her wish come true.
Be happy

Untold Emotions

First a finger, then a hand
Gripping the edge with whitened knuckles
A set of eyes peered over the edge
Curious eyes they were
Twinkling with mischievousness
Green eyes sparkling with untold emotions

Those eyes, wandering over the horizon
Across the endless expansion of the deep blue sea
Waves crashing upon jagged rocks
Sea foam misting her already tear-streaked face
Wind whipping her long brown hair around her
Like angels dancing, it floated in the wind
Her white dress in all its simplicity
Bound her legs like iron shackles

She pulled herself up to her bare feet
With arms spread like an eagle
Ready to take flight
She leapt off

Her pale body crashed upon the rocks
Like the sea in which she so dearly loved
Pent up emotions escaping
Like a condemned prisoner awaiting execution

To the Boy Whom I Adore

To the boy whom I adore,
Whose cheeks as radiant as ever;
His eyes that crinkle when he laughs
And form like the shape of a crescent moon.
Let me be the reason for your laughter

To the boy whom my heart belongs to,
Whose smile can make the flowers bloom,
Making me fluster so easily;
My heart gets filled with delight when he beams.
Let me be the one to protect it

To the boy who gives me butterflies,
Whose heart as delicate as mine,
And the one who fails to hold his tears;
He can never hide his true emotions.
Let me be the one to hold you

To the boy who had enchanted me,
Who doesn't appreciate his perfect body.
As small as a blossom he may be,
He always shines with ethereal beauty.
Let me kiss your insecurities away

To the boy who I'm writing this for,
Let me be the one to let you know
The things I've been longing to tell you—
I adore you, truly

Utopia

Every day is identical; a boundless routine
On my face only discourage and sorrow can be seen
Walking through the halls eyeing similar misery
We are all patients but of a different injury
All I can see is limitless blisters of different depths
And hear people's loud sighs and breaths
Listless beings roam my location
Every sound with a tone of hesitation
Trying to find out where their life is going
All these years with the current they were flowing,
Unknowingly we try to write
A future blindingly bright
Although we aren't the authors
And we're controlled by our fathers
We believe were imprisoned by our dismay
And forever chained by our life's disarray
Endeavouring to find a saviour
We go astray and learn inappropriate behaviour
To please our so called idols
We become our own rivals
Finding out who you really are
Isn't easy when expressing your opinion gave you a scar
We say were okay but we don't know
Without asking ourselves it doesn't show
We close our eyes and search deep
But all that's discovered is a melancholy seep
We try to seek aid but all we hear is scoff
So once again we shut ourselves off
How do we know joy when all we've ever felt
Is grief and despair is all we've ever dealt
Sceptical about every piece of advice

Since these days everyone heart is full of ice
You never know
Whether they're friends or foes
They might be acting like you're homies
But soon later you find out you were enemies
Nobody to trust but yourself
Cause nowadays everyone's loyalty is on the shelf
You know the real ones through a feeling
By their comfort you find healing
And by their loss you find anguish
And their happiness makes your glum vanish
They help you discover who you are
And take you places way too far
To be forgotten and left behind
They aid in starting your grind
But nothing lasts forever and so they leave
Confronting your loss, you bereave
You gave it your all but still have regrets
They left you without a chance to pay your debts
Although you're alone, you have your life together
You know what to do, no need for bather
All my remorse I shall toss
By moving on I became my own boss
You were born alone and that's how you'll always be
Soon enough you'll say I love me
For what I've been through defines who I am
Getting lost or involved in that scam
Nothing went to waste it's been a pleasure
All the heartache leads you to your treasure
So be patient and hold on tight
No matter what you go through you'll get stronger despite
No matter how lost you are
You'll find the way, life's bizarre

Be thankful for now
With that being said I shall bow

Childish

She may be lost
and just a little broken
But there's beauty in traveling,
Not knowing where you're going

Blindly treading
Humming along the way
Singing her own tunes
Creating her own beautiful day

Skipping, bouncing, hopping along
Childish in manner
She's a beautiful song

With no rhyme and rhythm
And no sense of beat
I think she's beautiful
With her two left feet

Numb to all the pain

I don't feel much pain after losing you
Got a knife in my heart
And stitches to put myself back together
Where did all the colour go
Every day is grey through my eyes
Remembering the times I held you tight to my chest never letting you go
Remembering the times you asked me to sing with my horrible voice
The times when I was the one living and not the devil on my shoulder

After losing you all pain became nothing
The broken bones after the fights
The knife that scarred my chest from top to bottom
The bitter taste of the crimson gushing out my chest and mouth
None of it existed because I am numb to life

My eyes that are seeing back then
My heart that was beating back then
Obsessed with the thought of having you back
The pain just grew and grew until I couldn't take it anymore
Taking one step forward to your voice
Then 2 steps back into my delusions

Feels like nobody understands
Feel so alone with a hole in my chest from depression
Can't seem to sleep peacefully because all I see
Is her image with crimson streaking down her body

I reach my hand out she disappears from my view
I yell but all I get is silence in return

Memories Fade

It's a slip of the mind
the murkiness of the mirage
something off in the distance
not quite a sensory memory,
yet I feel it across my fingers
on the edge of my lips
slithering through my soul.

There in the flash of the light
the fatal recall of emotion
closer than my own heartbeat
not quite a delicate whisper
sending chills through bones
caressing forgotten feelings
twisting the ties of my essence.

It's a dance of a dream
the slight of hand
inside the magician's illusion
not quite a visual feast,
yet I see you in my mind
taste you as we kiss
and miss you for all time.

Me, a storm, you, a light

i paint our pasts with my bedroom light off,
the flickering ghosts of street lights,
tiptoeing their frail arms into cracked windows,
but we were never built to last,
our ankles were never meant to support us.
only these hands, holding my body underwater,
could truly save the meaning of us.

And at noon, while the ground was still moist,
and the trees were still swaying, i bundled up feathers,
from dead ravens, from dead doves, and tied them to my hairs,
shut my eyes, and let my soul wander,
to where I was a bird, and you were a worm,
where the earth was void of sin,
and nothing else nurtured me more than you.
to the open sky and the now toss of trees,
to a dimple in earth, and my pebbled feet,
to you, drowning in a puddle of last night's storm.

My hair is falling out, and the birds are begging for their feathers back.

My window is latched shut,
the rain continues to drum against it,
you are almost painted, you are almost painted
but I am still a part of the storm, my body lives unfinished

Narcotic shame

Shame will kill you from the inside out
It's vile and deadly and filled with self-doubt
I hate being judged for mistakes that I've made
That's not who I am and the price has been paid
Addiction ruined my mind I couldn't think clear
Couldn't recognize my own face in the mirror
There's so many years I can't remember a bit
There's so many others I wish I could forget

Shame is disgusting it's toxic and necrotic
But I ingest it all like my favourite narcotic
It makes me so sick it aches in my bones
But it's all I have left that I truly own

This shame it seeps out of my every pore
Some days I just can't take it anymore
But I know myself I know that's not me
It's just something that happened unexpectedly

I want you to see me for who I really am
Then judge for yourself you'll see it's no scam
So please don't judge you don't know all the facts
We've all done things we wish we could take back

Rewind time

People always say if I could go back I'd never change a thing
I have no regrets cause my mistakes made me
I understand that I really do
But I would definitely go back and avoid meeting you

I wish I never ever saw your face
My life's been ruined my name disgraced
I've learned some things that's for sure
But I want my life back to the way things were

How did this happen it feels so surreal
This wasn't the plan this wasn't the deal
I don't understand how I got in so deep
They took my soul now it's theirs to keep

So I'd rewind time and never look your way
I'd go back to that very first day
Then I'd be free
me and my name would be clear
I'd be living my life like you were never here.

www.ingramcontent.com/pod-product-compliance
Lightning Source LLC
Chambersburg PA
CBHW031414040426
42444CB00005B/560